TEARS, LAUGHS, AND DREAMS

A POETRY COLLECTION

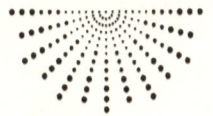

ALICIA RADES

To Nicole, who is an inspiration to everyone around her.

KISS YOU

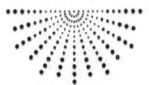

Kiss you.
Kiss you.
That's what I like to do
when I'm with you.
Baby, I want to,
and you do, too.
Kiss you.

WHILE I SMILE

Sometimes I can't see clearly.
Sometimes I lose my way.
Sometimes I don't know who I've hurt.
There's times when I just fade.
But I keep my pride,
don't hear what they say.
I hold my head up high
and don't let go of faith.

I've had some hard times,
and sometimes I cry,
but I hold on to hope
and know I'll survive.
I've let people down
and paid the price.
I hide my face and smile while I cry inside.

I JUST HATE

I hate that stupid laugh you have,
the way you flirt and you call me fat.
I hate the way you obsess
about nothing at all.
The way you fish for compliments,
it's obvious you're so jealous.
The way you act behind my back,
but you're so nice to my face.
There's so much about you
I just hate.

VICTIMS OF FATE

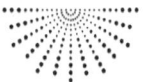

A POEM FROM JULIET TO ROMEO

It's like we couldn't avoid this,
preplanned all along.
We fell in love too soon.
Our expectations were wrong.
How did we get here?
How did things turn out this way?
Is it based on chance,
or have we and fate come face to face?

Is this what they call fate?
Does it have to end this way?
Can stars be rearranged?
Can the gods' minds be changed?
Does fate know me?
Am I a victim of its schemes?
Is this the end for you and me?

I wonder if it's true,
or if it's only in our dreams.
Is it really real?
Can you have a destiny?
And when will you know
when your time has finally come?
Is it at an end,
and is there any way to run?

Is this what they call fate?
Does it have to end this way?
Can stars be rearranged?
Can the gods' minds be changed?
Does fate know me?
Am I a victim of its schemes?
Is this the end for you and me?

Did fate decide on this
as you're lying on the floor?
I guess that I must die
to be with you one more.
I know that I can't
turn back the hands of time.
So with this dagger I must die
to be with my Romeo.

Is this what they call fate?

Does it have to end this way?
Can stars be rearranged?
Can the gods' minds be changed?
Does fate know me?
Am I a victim of its schemes?
Is this the end for you and me?

BLACK AND WHITE

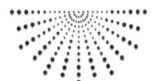

Every day is a new day.
That's what they told me.
I'm sick and tired of the same thing.
They call it routine,
but I really don't know.
Every day is a repeat.
Every step's in the same beat,
and it's really getting old.

I just want a change.
Every day's just the same.
I just want a change
and stop living in yesterday.
Mix it up. Put some color in my life.
I don't want to be living in
black and white.

Every day feels the same way,
nothing out of place.
I feel I'm in a dream.
It just keeps repeating.
I wish things were different.
I feel I'm on repeat,
but that's how life's taught me.
It's just wishful thinking.

I just want a change.
Every day's just the same.
I just want a change
and stop living in yesterday.
Mix it up. Put some color in my life.
I don't want to be living in
black and white.

WAVES OF LIFE

I'm riding on the waves of life,
crashing into the mountain side.
Feeling the rise of the tide,
I'm holding on just to survive.
I can feel the heat of the summer,
fighting hard, yet being pulled under.
Losing breath, I am drowning,
unfamiliar with these surroundings.
I made a promise to myself
that somehow I would make it out.
I won't give up—I'll make it through,
no matter what I have to do.
I'm being pulled by the current.
Don't cry for me 'cause I can do it.

DRAWN TO SIZE

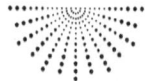

It feels like I've been shrunk down
into almost nothing,
left without detail,
but there's really something
hidden out of sight,
too small to see with your eyes.
Maybe if you paid attention
you could see
this is just the smallest part of me.

If you could see
every piece of me,
you'd know there's more than it seems.
If you would stop
shrinking me down,

making me feel small,
you could see me right,
if I were drawn to size.

WHILE I'M DOWN

You've never given me the chance
to fight back.
I won't use your sick and twisted ways.
I just want to communicate.
You've never given me the chance
to tell you how I feel.
I'll take my time right now
to tell you everything I never said.

Why you gotta kick me while I'm down?
Why you gotta make me feel so small?
Isn't there a better way to deal with pain
than taking it out on me
just because I look as if I'm weak?
Please tell me why I'm the one to be blamed.

IN MY SHOES

You look at me.
I've got it so easy.
You only believe
what you can see.
There's so much I don't show.
There's so much you don't know.

Here are my shoes.
Walk around for a while.
Come back and tell me
that you never tripped and fell.
The runway's not the place for you.
It's not that easy in my shoes.

Sure, from the outside
it looks so elegant,

but when you're not perfect,
it's so easy to pretend.
The blisters cause pain,
but no one else is noticing.

Here are my shoes.
Walk around for a while.
Come back and tell me
that you never tripped and fell.
The runway's not the place for you.
It's not that easy in my shoes.

I'm sure you can't be comfortable,
but you look more comfortable than me.
I'm sure you fall sometimes, too,
but I just can't see.

Here are my shoes.
Walk around for a while.
Come back and tell me
that you never tripped and fell.
The runway's not the place for you.
It's not that easy in my shoes.

WHERE IS MY FAITH?

Where is my faith in you?
Everything's gone wrong.
Everything's gone wrong.

I put my trust in your hands.
Now you've torn it to pieces.
So where's my faith, you ask.
You've got blood stains on your hands.
You've got blood stains on your hands.

NO REGRETS

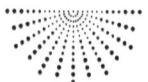

You can't hold on to a grudge or the past.
You've got to make each moment last.
To live life to the fullest,
you can't regret a single moment.
You've got to learn to forgive and forget,
and live life with no regrets.

WHEN WE SMILE

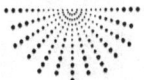

There's no point in living in regret
or dwelling in denial.
The tears we cry are different
when we smile.

SIGNIFICANT COLORS

My world is black and white
with dark and bolded lines.
No color to fill the empty space,
no brilliant colors to lighten up my day.
It's like I'm color blind,
or like the rainbow's lost in time.

So can you paint me a picture
with significant colors?
Lighten the world with red and pink,
blue and orange, turquoise and green.
Bring some flavor to my life.
Paint me a picture
with significant colors.

STANDING OVATION

My eyes are always moving,
and you think that I can't see.
You think that I don't notice, but I do.

You put in so much effort,
and you hear no applause,
but here I am applauding you.

To the girl who tries her hardest
to make her parents proud,
the one who cries herself to sleep
because they're not around.

To the girl who's suffering
from a broken heart,

the one who offers up a shoulder
and never falls apart.

Each one of you deserves recognition.
This is my standing ovation.

LIGHT

The only light we cannot see
is the one inside ourselves.
So shine a little brighter
and let it out.

BROKEN

I see you're trying to run away.
You're scared, you're so afraid.
Trying to hide your confusion,
afraid to admit that you are losing.
And baby, you're slipping.
You keep on tripping,
but baby, I believe in you.

So don't hide, Broken,
and don't you ever forget.
I know that you're afraid,
and you don't know what to do,
but don't break, Broken,
because I love you.

CHASING RAINBOWS

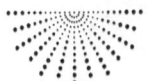

The only thing we cannot reach is the horizon,
and yes it's true we can touch the sky.
We can grab hold of a rainbow,
and soon enough we'll find Paradise.
We have proof there is something out there.
Just look up at the stars tonight.
Love is the closest thing to magic.
There's more than it seems to life.

Don't let go of that rainbow.
Chase any star you'd like.
Don't let doubt stop you.
Keep your faith in line.
Take hold of those dreams of yours
'cause you're unstoppable.

Don't let them tell you different.
Life's not impossible.

SHINE

Misconceptions judge you.
It seems nobody loves you,
but a smile escapes
to get you through the day
as faces turn away
to criticize your every move.
But you don't let it get to you.

Leave the words unheard.
The dirty looks were never seen.
Let your internal fire
shine a little brighter.
One step at a time, live your life,
and let your heart and soul shine.

Laughs are directed at you.

No one's laughing with you.
Faith's the only hand you have to hold,
so you hold a little tighter
to show them you are happy with yourself.

Leave the words unheard.
The dirty looks were never seen.
Let your internal fire
shine a little brighter.
One step at a time, live your life,
and let your heart and soul shine.

THIS ISN'T OVER

You're walking along
down the middle of the railroad tracks
on the north side of town.
You're wondering if they ever end
or if they just keep going.
You're trying to sort out everything on your
    mind, and then you realize:

This isn't over until you turn your face
and walk away.
Sometimes you trip.
Sometimes you fall.
Sometimes you get up.
Sometimes you stay down.
It's not over until you go,
say you're done and walk back home.

THIS IS WHY I WRITE

I started writing for the ring of rhyme.
I poured my heart out with every line.
I sang my words for most my life
but shifted course to freelance write.

I wrote for pennies but didn't care,
although others said it wasn't fair.
But I didn't give in; I didn't agree
'cause it wasn't about the money to me.

This gave me a chance to explore my talents,
to learn and grow throughout the challenge.

I don't care if I'm writing stories or songs
or poems or blog posts for hours long

because whatever I write and wherever I go,
writing is still a part of my soul.

IMPOSSIBLE

They say that it's impossible
to turn back the hands of time.
They say it can't be done,
but has anybody tried?

They say that it's impossible,
on the moon you can't survive.
They say it can't be done,
but has anybody tried?

They say that it's impossible,
a city cannot hide.
They say it can't be done,
but has anybody tried?

They say that it's impossible

to live a two-hundred year life.
They say it can't be done,
but has anybody tried?

They say that it's impossible,
but we'll hold our heads up high.
What never could be done,
now we're gonna try.

YOUR SMILE

I hope you can work up the courage
so you can fight your fears.
I hope no one convinces you
you're too big to cry those tears.
I hope you never lose your faith
on what truly matters in life.
I hope you never lose yourself.
I hope you always do what's right.

I want to catch you whenever you fall.
I want to be there when no one else is at all.
I hope you can trust me with holding your heart.
I'll never break it. I promised that from the start.
I hope so much for you, but most of all,
I hope you never lose your smile.

ORDINARY

I don't want to be told who I am
when I already know.
I don't want to be told what to do
whenever I don't,
and I don't want to be told who
I should be.
Don't want to be a clone
from a magazine.

I don't want to be ordinary.
I'd rather be unique.
I don't want to fit into the crowd
or be compared to someone else.
I just want to be myself.

EVERYBODY CRIES

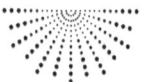

I see your eyes. I see you fake that smile.
You hide behind your lies,
tell the world that you are fine.
Nobody cares. Nobody understands.
There's pain you have to bear.
Sometimes you feel you can't.

You need to know that everybody cries.
Everyone has a secret to hide.
The pain that you are feeling,
you think no one else knows.
I'm begging you please just don't let go.
This life is tough, it's hard to do,
but someone else knows what you're going
    through.

WE'LL WATCH YOU SHINE

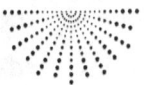

Your eyes are stained with tears.
You think no one can see, but we can all hear
everything that you're not saying.
You're broken inside,
and we can all see your light's diminishing.
Don't let go. We want you to know:

That we'll be there when you're ready to shine,
in the front row, blinded by the light
held behind those tear-stained eyes.
Whenever you're ready,
we'll watch you shine.

Take your time.
We can wait here patiently.
This heartbreak will pass

if you just keep waiting.
Just stay strong.
We're here when everything goes wrong.

And we'll be there when you're ready to shine,
in the front row, blinded by the light
held behind those tear-stained eyes.
Whenever you're ready,
we'll watch you shine.

Don't let it fade.
Your eyes are shining brighter every day.
Keep your faith.
Hold your head up high.
Don't listen to what they say.
We're gonna keep you safe.

We'll be there when you're ready to shine,
in the front row, blinded by the light
held behind those tear-stained eyes.
Whenever you're ready,
we'll watch you shine.

TAKE ME AS I AM

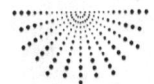

I am not perfect,
but take me as I am.
We all have a weakness,
but I do the best I can.
I work and find the time to play
and do my best academically.
I try to fit everything into one day,
but it can be a bit hard for me.
I'm trying to do my best.
I hope that's good enough.
I'm keeping up my confidence.
I'm trying to stay tough.
Please don't judge my imperfections.
I'm doing all I can.
I am not perfect,
but please take me as I am.

WHEN I'M GONE

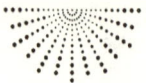

What will they say when I'm not around to hear?
Will they call me just a pretty face,
or will they have better things to say?

What will they say about me when I'm gone?
Will they call me someone,
or just forget my name?

Well, I don't want to be forgotten.
I want someone to know
that I'm not just a stone.

And I won't be
just measured in square feet.
There's so much more to me,
and I'll let everybody see.

What will they do in ten years down the road?
Will they read the words I left behind,
or will they be too hard to find?

What will they do when I'm not here to see?
Will they look at pictures of me,
or just use them as firewood?

Well, I don't want to be forgotten.
I want someone to know
that I'm not just a stone.

And I won't be
just measured in square feet.
There's so much more to me,
and I'll let everybody see.

MOVED ON

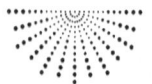

There were tears and laughs and dreams,
and everything that's in between.
Now all that's left is memories.
I've moved on to better things.
I heard you're doing okay.
I am, too, by the way.
I've stopped dreaming of you.
I hope you've moved on from me, too.

I'm not the same girl you used to know.
I've changed so much since you let go.
I've fixed my faults and found the truth,
the girl I didn't know when I knew you.
I've found a man who fits just right
into my new amazing life.

Time has changed, and so have I.
I'm different since you said goodbye.
I've been transformed and turned out fine.
It just took a little time.
But my wounds healed and my broken heart,
but that doesn't mean there aren't any scars.

Nothing can replace you.
It's impossible to do,
but that doesn't mean I haven't moved on,
even though your memory isn't gone.

There were tears and laughs and dreams,
and everything that's in between.
Now all that's left is memories.
I've moved on to better things.
I heard you're doing okay.
I am, too, by the way.
I've stopped dreaming of you.
I hope you've moved on from me, too.

ANOTHER CHAPTER

Time moves on.
You've gotta say goodbye.
You can't hold on to this forever.
All you take when you leave
is a heart full of memories
and a suitcase full of your old things.

Standing in the front yard,
kissing your childhood goodbye,
your mother starts to cry.
She doesn't want to let you go,
but it's a sacrifice required
if she wants to see you grow.

This is the time to find where you belong.

No turning back, no holding on.
This is the time,
another chapter of your life.

HERE'S TO

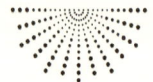

It's almost time
to say goodbye
to everything I once knew,
everything but you.
It's almost time
to begin a new life,
everything left behind,
everything but you.

Here's to everything we dreamed of.
Don't ever let your dreams go.
I'm here, always beside you.
I'll help you reach every goal.
Here's to the start of something new.
Here's to me and you.

Goodbye, my childhood.
Hello, the rest of my life.
I'm a little scared,
but it all feels just right,
like this is where I'm meant to be,
like this is supposed to be happening.

Here's to everything we dreamed of.
Don't ever let your dreams go.
I'm here, always beside you.
I'll help you reach every goal.
Here's to the start of something new.
Here's to me and you.

ROMANCES

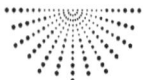

If I could pick the perfect scenes
from the perfect romances,
if I could make our love
just like Shakespeare imagined,
if I could pick and choose
the ones for me and you:

We'd fall in love like Juliet and Romeo.
We'd be as carefree as Jack and Rose.
We'd share a perfect kiss
like the frog and princess,
and then like Ally and Noah,
we'd lie down by each other.
We'd hold each other's hands
and die together.

HOLDING ON

These pages are blank.
My words are unspoken.
The lyrics are wrong.
A soul you can't open.
The only sound you can hear
is the strum of my guitar,
and if you listen to it closely,
you can hear the offbeat of my heart.

Tears that keep me from falling asleep.
My heart keeps you in my dreams.
My soul keeps hanging on to you.
No doubt I won't let go soon.
Words I can't seem to write,
thoughts that keep me up all night.
My last words are true:

I'll be holding on to you.

Promises I kept
are the ones you couldn't keep.
I told you I'd stay here
through everything.
No matter what the trial,
I'd be there to pull you through,
but now I'm the one
who needs help from you.

Tears that keep me from falling asleep.
My heart keeps you in my dreams.
My soul keeps hanging on to you.
No doubt I won't let go soon.
Words I can't seem to write,
thoughts that keep me up all night.
My last words are true:
I'll be holding on to you.

You told me you'd protect me
from anyone who'd hurt me.
You want to know the truth?
You should have been protecting me from you.

Tears that keep me from falling asleep.
My heart keeps you in my dreams.

My soul keeps hanging on to you.
No doubt I won't let go soon.
Words I can't seem to write,
thoughts that keep me up all night.
My last words are true:
I'll be holding on to you.

JUST YOU

Any guy can hold my hand,
but no one can hold it like you do.
Anyone can kiss my lips,
but no one can kiss just like you.
Anyone can say, "I love you,"
but it holds no meaning to me.
So when I say, "I miss you,"
it's who you are—not what I want someone else
    to be.

Any guy can make me laugh,
but not the way I do with you.
Anyone can make me smile,
but not the way you used to.
Anyone can call me beautiful,
but I feel perfect when you say it.

Anyone can steal my heart,
but only you can get away with it.

Any guy can drive me wild,
but not insane like you do.
Any guy can make me cry,
but not as much as I did for you.

It's you I miss.
It's you I love.
It's you I need
and I dream of.
Not the thought
of someone to be true,
or someone to hold me.
It's just you.

CARDS

You said that we would roll the dice,
let the chips fall where they may.
You said that if we played it right,
we would win this game.

But this doesn't feel like chance at all
or that we're coming out ahead.
You've got secrets in your pocket.
You're playing those cards instead.

The devil deals the cards,
and you're playing on his side.
You thought no one could see
what you're trying to hide.

You thought that you could cheat the house,
but baby, I'm not blind.
You may think you understand the game,
but it's my deal this time.

THE IMPOSSIBLE

If I could, I'd buy you the moon.
I'd arrange the stars to spell out *I love you*.
I'd move mountains with my bare hands.
I'd turn a piece of glass back into sand.
I'd split the seas so you could cross,
walk around the world just because.

I'd stop breathing for hours,
give you a super power.
I'd change the sky to pink,
make red the color green.
And smells would taste like sound.
I'd turn the world upside down.

I would do the impossible

just so you would know
that I'd do anything
just to show you
how much I love you.
I'd do the impossible for you.

MY HERO

You're always there,
always around
to catch me right before I hit the ground.
You're always next to me.
You give me strength when I'm weak.
You give me hope when I give up.
You keep me here. You give me love.

You always know what to say.
The words you use give me faith.
The way you smile, I can't explain.
The look in your eyes gives me away.
You know exactly how to hold me.
You know the way things should be.

You always know what words to use

to always keep me next to you.
You know exactly how to touch me
so the softest touch tells me you love me.
You know exactly how to kiss me
to make sure I'll never leave.

When I fall you're there to catch me.
You give me air when I'm suffocating.
You're always there to wipe my tears.
When I scream, you're close enough to hear.
You always hold me so close
at times I need you the most.
You're by my side to see
that you're everything to me.
You love me enough to know
that you're my hero.

JUST LIKE YOU

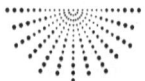

I am not the kind of girl
you'd find wearing high heels.
I prefer my bare feet in the grass.

I am not the kind of girl
you'd find wearing miniskirts.
I prefer a t-shirt and jeans.

I am not the kind of girl
who parties on the weekend.
I'd rather spend my time with you.

This is why you love me.
It's why you think I'm cute.
 This is why you love me.
'Cause I'm just like you with boobs.

MAYBE IT'S A DREAM

So maybe this is the most vivid dream
I've ever had.
Maybe it's the realest thing
that will ever last.
Maybe I'll awake
to find things didn't turn out this way.
I'd wish I could sleep for one more day.

Maybe this is just a dream,
just a vivid fantasy.
But baby, if it's love,
I don't want to wake up.
Maybe I'm just dreaming,
but maybe it's the real thing.

WARRIOR

You saw your chance.
You took my hand,
showed me what the world was like,
how to live with an open mind.
I was just a little girl on my own.

Now what is in front of me
is what you taught me to be.
I am so thankful for that.

I couldn't have done this without you.
I couldn't make it on my own.
I make break and I may bleed,
but I'm stronger than I've ever been.
You made me a warrior.

I LOVE THE LITTLE THINGS

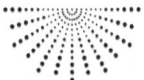

I love it when you wake up.
Your hair is sticking straight up.
Your smile's unlike anything.
It makes my heart skip a beat.

I love it when you're talking.
You lean over and kiss me.
You interrupt yourself
just to make me smile.

I love it when we sit there.
You're playing with my hair.
You're talking about nothing
just to talk to me.

I love it when you hold me.

I love how much you know me.
I love it when you say,
"Forever and ever."

I love the little things.
The simple things, they're everything.
I love the little things,
because the little things say everything.

THEME SONG

Your voice is the lyrics.
Your face is the music.
Every part fits perfectly
as if your smile were the melody.
Your heartbeat keeps the time.
Your eyes make everything rhyme.

You're the song I could never write
that I've waited for my whole live.
You're the song I could never sing.
I couldn't perfect a single thing.
You're the song I need to hear
that wipes away all of my tears.
You're the song I've waited for forever.
Music, lyrics—it all its perfectly together.

OH, BABY

Oh, baby, do you know what you did?
You've got me hanging by a thread.
I can't stop thinking 'bout you.
I've got you in my head.

Oh, baby, I've got you on my mind.
Don't you know I think about you all the time?
I can't fight this feeling.
I know it's real and true.
Baby, I love you.

Oh, baby, you're one of a kind.
Don't you know I dream about you every night?
I can't fight this feeling.
I know it's real and true.
Baby, I love you.

THE LITTLE THINGS

I love the way you love everything about me,
the way you kiss me when we say hello,
the way you smile when you're genuinely happy.
You squeeze me so tight, you might break a bone.

I love your eyes when you're staring at me.
You move my bangs away from my face.
Suddenly, time stops when our eyes lock,
and the rest of the world all fades away.

Baby, I love everything about you.
No, you're not perfect, but you're perfect for me.
Baby, I love everything about you,
but most of all, I love the little things.

I love it when you tell me I look beautiful

even when I know that I don't.
I love the way you play with my hair.
You hold my hand when you're driving me home.

I love it when we take naps together,
and we crawl under the sheets.
I lay my head on your chest.
I love the feel of your bare feet.

Baby, I love everything about you.
No, you're not perfect, but you're perfect for me.
Baby, I love everything about you,
but most of all, I love the little things.

MAGIC TO ME

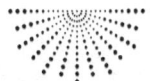

It's not fair,
the way you look tonight.
You're standing there.
What a beautiful sight.
With your t-shirt on,
your muscles defined.
I'm not this strong
to keep you off my mind.

You don't have to try.
It's all natural.
This feeling here tonight,
it's magical.
You may not believe it,
but baby, I can see it.
You are magic—magic to me.

EYES WIDE OPEN

Eyes wide open,
scared of what I'll lose if I close them.
I've got so much to lose,
and I don't want to be without you.

So I'll keep my eyes wide open.
I'll cherish you with every moment.
I'll hold you tight, treat you right,
and make every second count—
with my eyes wide open.

WITH ALL MY HEART

There are so many things I love,
but some just can't compare.
I love it when the sun shines
and when the wind blows through my hair.
I love when people smile.
I love it when it rains.
I love the sound of music
whenever it gets played.
I love to sing and dance.
I love the smell of pie.
I love to see the wonders held
in someone else's eye.
I love the cry of kittens.
I love when thunder starts.
But most of all I love *you*
with ALL of my heart.

ABOUT THE AUTHOR

Alicia Rades has been writing poetry since the age of eight. She wrote most of her poems between the ages of fourteen and seventeen in the form of song lyrics. After many years, she decided to put together her best works of poetry in this book. In addition to writing poetry, Alicia is a USA Today bestselling author of young adult and new adult paranormal books.